The Constitution in Plain English

Chris Kozak

© 2017 Chris Kozak

Many thanks to my wife, Grace, and to my mother, Juanita Kozak.

I would also like to thank the following professors for the impact they have had on my legal education, and therefore, on this book: Michael Farris, Brad Gideon, Glen Staszewski, Frank Ravitch, Cynthia Lee Starnes, Stephanie LaRose, Bridgette Carr, Suellyn Scarnecchia, Elizabeth Campbell, James M. Chen, Kristi L. Bowman, Michael Lawrence, Mark Totten, Jennifer Rosa, Phillip Pucillo, Ann Sherman, Daniel D. Barnhizer, Brian Kalt, Judge David W. McKeague, and Kevin Saunders.

This book is dedicated to Dean James S. Ruebel and Mrs. Connie Ruebel, for their kindness and their love of learning.

The Constitution in Plain English

Introduction

The Constitution is a cryptic beast. Lawyers, law professors, and law students spend an absurd amount of time learning what it does mean and arguing about what they think it should mean. To make matters worse, the Founders decided not to integrate Amendments into the original text of the Constitution. Instead, they simply listed them afterward. The Supreme Court, led by some of the best and brightest lawyers in the history of our country, has still struggled to give precise and consistent meaning to its words.

In order to make it easier for lawyers and citizens to understand what the Constitution currently means, the Library of Congress publishes annual editions of a book compiling and synthesizing cases interpreting the Constitution.[1] That book—perhaps more aptly described as a tome—currently clocks in at 2,840 pages. It is an indispensable reference guide for lawyers, judges, and the ambitious citizen, but is profoundly unhelpful for normal people who just want to know what the Constitution generally means.

The point of this (small) book is to show that the general principles of the Constitution are generally not as complicated as lawyers sometimes make them out to be. Indeed, the Founders—who were committed to government by the People—intended for all citizens to

---

[1] LIBRARY OF CONGRESS, *The Constitution of the United States of America: Analysis and Interpretation* (Government Printing Office, Centennial ed. 2013), *available digitally at* www.congress.gov/constitution-annotated/#. The document is also available in the Apple Store or through Google Play.

understand the Constitution simply by reading it. But after 200+ years of amendment and interpretation, that task has become almost impossible. My goal is to translate the Constitution's text (and subtext) into modern, plain English, so that the everyday citizen can understand the governing principles of our country.

A word of caution: There is a reason that the Library of Congress's treatise is almost 3,000 pages long. Many areas of the law *are* quite complicated. This book is meant to act as a sort of "pocket guide" to the Constitution, and not as legal advice or an authoritative guide to what the law means in a particular case. For that reason, it is not a substitute for the advice of a competent attorney. If you need a lawyer, you can contact your State's bar association or visit a reputable online lawyer search tool such as *avvo.com* or *findlaw.com*.

-C.K.

The Constitution in Plain English

PREAMBLE

We the People of the United States, in order to form a more perfect union, establish justice, ensure domestic peace, provide for the national defense, promote our general welfare, and secure the blessings of liberty to ourselves and our children, do create and establish this Constitution for the United States of America.

PART ONE
The Legislative Branch

Section 1: The Legislative Power of the United States

Clause 1: Location. All legislative powers of the United States shall reside solely in Congress. Congress shall consist of the Senate and the House of Representatives.

Clause 2: Definition. The Legislative Power of the United States is the power to express the common will of the People by laws passed through the procedures described in this Constitution.

Clause 3: Limitation. The Legislative Power shall only extend to the subjects specifically named in this Constitution. All power not given to Congress resides in the States and the People, respectively, unless this Constitution specifically says otherwise.

Section 2: The U.S. House of Representatives

Clause 1: Structure. The House of Representatives shall be composed of members chosen every two years by the people of each state. Each member shall have one vote. The House of Representatives shall have the power to select its Speaker and other Officers.

Clause 2: Qualifications. In order to serve as a Representative, a person must be twenty-five years old, have been a citizen of the United States for seven years, and be a resident of the state he or she represents.

Clause 3: Number of Representatives. Each state shall have at least one representative. However, the states may have additional representatives in proportion to their respective population, counting the whole number of persons in each state (except for Native Americans who are not taxed). Every ten years, Congress shall adjust by law the number of members each state receives in the House of Representatives, in light of the census. But if a state denies any citizen or citizens the right to vote in any federal or state election—except for acts of rebellion or other felonies—then their representation in Congress shall be reduced by the number of citizens whose right to vote has been denied.

Clause 4: Vacancies. If a representative dies or resigns, the Governor of their State shall fill the vacancy until the next election.

Section 3: The U.S. Senate

Clause 1: Structure. The United States Senate shall be composed of two senators from each state, elected by the people of the state. Each Senator shall have one vote. The Vice President of the United States shall be the President of the Senate, but may only vote to break a tie. The Senate shall have the power to choose their other officers, including the person who will serve as the President of the Senate in the Vice President's absence.

Clause 2: Qualifications. In order to serve as a Senator, a person must be thirty years old, have been a citizen of the United States for nine years, and be a resident of the state he or she represents.

Clause 3: Terms. Each Senator shall be elected for a six-year term. However, the Senators shall be divided as equally as possible into three classes, so that approximately one-third of the Senate is elected every two years.

Clause 3: Vacancies. If a Senator dies or resigns, the Governor of their State shall fill the vacancy. However, the legislature of any state may by law provide for a special election for the replacement of the temporary Senator.

Section 4: Elections

Clause 1: Election Rules. The times, places, and rules of elections for Senators and Representatives shall be prescribed by the legislature of each state. However, Congress may by law make or alter such regulations for any reason.

Clause 2: The Right to Vote. If a citizen is eighteen years of age or older, then they shall have the right to vote in state and federal elections. This right shall not be denied or restricted because of race, color, sex, age (for citizens over eighteen years of age), previous condition of servitude, or failure to pay any tax. Congress shall have power to enforce these rights by appropriate legislation.

Clause 3: Power Transfer. The terms of Senators and Representatives shall end at noon on January 3rd, and the terms of their successors shall begin. Congress must assemble at least once per year on January 3rd; however, Congress may by law select a different day.

The Constitution in Plain English

Section 5: Internal Rules

Clause 1: Internal Governance. The House and the Senate shall be the sole judge of the qualifications of their own members, to the extent not specified in this Constitution. The House and the Senate shall have power to compel the presence of absent members. Each house may create rules for their own hearings, punish members for disorderly conduct, and may expel a member by a two-thirds vote.

Clause 2: The Congressional Record. Each house shall keep a record of its proceedings. The record shall be made available to the public except in cases where secrecy is required. If one-fifth of members present request, the votes of each member shall be entered into the record.

Clause 3: Adjournment. Neither house shall adjourn for more than three days without the consent of the other, nor shall either house conduct official business outside the Capitol building in Washington, D.C.

Section 6: Compensation & Conflicts of Interest

Clause 1: Compensation. Senators and Representatives shall be paid a fixed salary as designated by law. However, no law changing this compensation shall take effect until an election of representatives has intervened.

Clause 2: Immunity. Except for acts of treason, felonies, or breaches of the peace, members of Congress shall be immune from arrest or detention while attending, traveling to, and returning from sessions of Congress.

Clause 3: Conflicts of Interest. No Senator or Representative shall hold any other office under the United States during his or her term in Congress.

Section 7: Legislation

Clause 1: Generally. Congress shall exercise the Legislative Power of the United States through legislation under this section.

Clause 2: Special Rules for Increasing Taxes. All bills proposing tax increases shall originate in the House of Representatives, but the Senate may propose amendments to such bills.

Clause 3: Passing Legislation. In order to pass legislation, an identical bill must be approved by a majority vote of both the Senate and the House of Representatives.

Clause 4: Presidential Signature or Veto. All bills that have passed in the House and the Senate shall be presented to the President. If the President signs the bill, then it becomes a Law. However, the President may veto a bill, and if so, he or she must state their objections to the bill and return it to Congress. If the President does not veto the bill within ten days, it becomes a law without his or her signature, unless Congress adjourns during that period.

Clause 5: Override. The last house to consider the vetoed bill shall record the President's objections in their record. If two-thirds of each house vote to override the veto, then the bill shall become a Law without the President's signature. However, in such cases, the votes of each member must be entered into the record.

Section 8: Impeachment

Clause 1: The Power. Congress shall have power to impeach any executive or judicial officer of the United States. A conviction following impeachment shall only cause the person convicted to be removed from office and to be disqualified from holding any position of trust in the federal government. However, the person convicted may also be subject to criminal prosecution according to the laws of the United States.

Clause 2: Impeachment. The House shall have the sole power to impeach by a majority vote of its members.

Clause 3: Trial. The Senate shall have the sole power to try all impeachments, and no person shall be convicted by less than a two-thirds vote of Senators present. When the Senate tries an impeachment, they must be under oath. If the President of the United States is tried, the Chief Justice shall preside over the trial.

Section 9: Powers of Congress

Clause 1: Scope of the Legislative Power. Congress shall have power to make laws that are appropriate and plainly intended to:
- (1) Carry out the powers granted to the government or officers of the United States by this Constitution; and
- (2) Protect the individual rights guaranteed by this Constitution from government interference.

Clause 2: Direct Taxes. Congress shall have power to issue and collect taxes on commercial goods, so long as such taxes are uniform throughout the United States.

Clause 3: Income Taxes. Congress shall have power to issue and collect taxes on all income, without regard to uniformity among the states or the population.

Clause 4: Borrowing & Spending. Congress shall have power to borrow money on the credit of the United States. Congress shall also have power to spend borrowed money or taxes raised in order to provide for the national defense and general welfare of the United States. However, no money shall be spent except as provided by law, and Congress shall provide to the public a routine accounting of the public expenditures.

Clause 5: Interstate & Foreign Commerce. Congress shall have power to regulate interstate commerce, foreign commerce, and commerce with Native American tribes. This power shall include the authority to regulate and protect the channels of such commerce, the objects and persons in such commerce, and any activity that—if aggregated nationally—would have a substantial effect on such commerce.

Clause 6: Immigration. Congress shall have exclusive power to create immigration laws and create uniform rules of naturalization.

Clause 7: Bankruptcy. Congress shall have exclusive power to create uniform bankruptcy laws for the United States.

Clause 8: National Currency. Congress shall have exclusive power to create and regulate currency, fix the standards of measurement, and punish counterfeiting.

Clause 9: United States Postal Service. Congress shall have exclusive power to establish and regulate a national post office system.

Clause 10: Intellectual Property. In order to promote the progress of the Arts & Sciences, Congress shall have exclusive power to grant authors and inventors the exclusive rights to their work for a limited time.

Clause 11: International & Maritime Law. Congress shall have exclusive power to define and punish piracy, crimes committed at sea, and crimes against the Law of Nations.

Clause 12: Declaring War. Congress shall have exclusive power to declare war, authorize the civilian capture of enemy ships, and provide the rules of military engagement.

Clause 13: The Armed Forces. Congress shall have exclusive power to establish and regulate the army, navy, air force, militia, national guard, and other military units of the United States, and to call them into service to suppress rebellions or repel invasions. However, no appropriation of money for the military may be for longer than two years.

Clause 14: District of Columbia. Congress shall have exclusive power to make laws governing the District of Columbia, which shall be the capital of the United States.

Clause 15: Territories. The Congress shall have power to make laws governing all the territories of the United States.

Section 10: Slavery & Involuntary Servitude

Clause 1: Prohibition. Neither slavery nor involuntary servitude shall exist in the United States or in any place subject to its jurisdiction, except as specific punishment for a crime where the party has been lawfully convicted.

Clause 2: Scope. This section extends to all acts—private and public—and applies regardless of whether the act was approved by any government. Congress shall have power make laws appropriate and plainly intended to enforce this section.

Section 11: Individual Rights

Clause 1: Freedom of Religion. Neither Congress nor any State shall establish or favor any religion. Neither shall they restrict the free exercise of any person's religion.

Clause 2: Freedom of Speech, Press, and Assembly. Neither Congress nor any state shall restrict the freedom of speech, punish a person for expressing their opinions, censor the press, prohibit any person from associating with those who share similar beliefs, or prevent any person from peacefully assembling, protesting, or demanding government action. However, the government may place reasonable time, place, and method restrictions on the exercise of this right.

Clause 3: Freedom to Bear Arms. Neither Congress nor any state shall place unreasonable restrictions on the People's right to keep and bear arms.

Clause 4: Privileges & Immunities. Neither Congress nor any State shall make or enforce any law treating the citizens of one state differently than the citizens of another state.

Clause 5: Equal Protection. Neither Congress nor any state shall discriminate against any person or group of persons based on their race, color, religious or moral beliefs, national origin, ancestry, gender, age, disability, veteran status, income, or citizenship.

Clause 6: Marriage. Neither Congress nor any state shall restrict a person's freedom to choose whom to marry or to construct a family in the way they choose.

Clause 7: Intimate Behavior. Neither Congress nor any state shall have the authority to punish private, consensual intimate behavior.

Clause 8: Children. Neither Congress nor any state shall involuntarily sterilize any person or prevent them from procreating as they choose. Nor shall any government restrict a parent's right to direct the upbringing and education of their child.

Clause 9: Abortion. Neither Congress nor any state shall unduly burden access to abortion. Neither shall any government restrict public access to contraception or otherwise intervene in a person's decision not to have a child.

Clause 10: Ex Post Facto Laws. Neither Congress nor any State shall punish an act that was legal when it occurred.

Clause 11: Bills of Attainder. Neither Congress nor any State shall pass a law singling out a person or group of persons and declaring them guilty of a crime.

Section 12: Restrictions on Individual Rights

Clause 1: Exceptions. The individual rights listed in Section 11 are not absolute. However, the government may restrict the exercise of these rights only as described in this section.

Clause 2: Strict Scrutiny. The rights described in Clause 2 (Speech, Press, & Assembly), Clause 5 (as to race, color, religion, national origin, and ancestry), and Clauses 6-9 (Marriage, intimate behavior, children, and abortion) may not be abridged unless the government shows that it is pursuing a compelling public interest that cannot be achieved by any less-intrusive means.

Clause 2: Intermediate Scrutiny. The rights described in Clause 5 (as to gender and citizenship status) and in Clause 3 (arms) may not be abridged unless the government shows that it is pursuing an important public interest and that the challenged policy is substantially related to that interest.

Clause 3: Free Exercise of Religion. Neutral and generally applicable laws are not unconstitutional merely because they have the incidental effect of burdening religious freedom.

Clause 4: Establishment of Religion. A law favoring or targeting a religion is unconstitutional unless it has a non-religious purpose, the principal effect of the law does not advance or inhibit religion, and does not result in excessive government entanglement with religion.

Clause 5: Rational Basis. All other laws are constitutional under this section unless they are arbitrary, irrational, or completely unrelated to a legitimate government interest.

Section 13: Restrictions on Congress's Authority

Clause 1: Habeas Corpus. Any person detained by the United States or any State shall have the right to petition a federal court for a writ of habeas corpus, alleging that his or her detention violates this Constitution or the laws of the United States. If the detention is unlawful, the Court shall order the person's release. Congress shall not suspend the writ, except in cases of rebellion or public safety.

Clause 2: Housing Soldiers. In times of peace, Congress shall not compel citizens to feed and house soldiers in their homes. In times of war, Congress may do so, but only by law.

Clause 3: Export Taxes. Congress shall not place any tax or duty on goods exported from any state.

Clause 4: Titles of Nobility. Neither Congress nor any State shall grant a title of Nobility, and no person holding a state or federal office shall accept any title of Nobility from a foreign state without the consent of Congress.

Section 14: Restrictions on State Authority

Clause 1: International Law. No state shall enter into a treaty, alliance, confederation. Nor shall any state enter into any other agreement or compact with another state or a foreign government without the consent of Congress.

Clause 2: Military Operations. No state shall, without the consent of Congress, declare war or commit any act of war unless the State is in such imminent danger that it cannot wait for the U.S. military to intervene.

Clause 3: Taxes. No state shall, without the consent of Congress, tax imports and exports, except for what is strictly necessary for enforcing its inspection laws. All laws passed under this section shall be subject to the revision and control of Congress.

Clause 4: Miscellaneous Prohibitions. No state shall coin money or recognize any currency anything except for silver, gold, and the U.S. dollar. No state shall pass any law impairing contractual obligations.

The Constitution in Plain English

PART TWO
The President & The Executive Branch

Section 1: The Executive Power of the United States

Clause 1: Location. The Executive Power of the United States shall reside in the President. The President shall receive a salary during his or her term in office, which shall not be changed during that term. While the President is in office, he shall not receive compensation from any other source.

Clause 2: Definition. The Executive Power of the United States is (a) the authority to enforce and administer the laws of the United States, (b) the duty to represent the interests of the United States abroad, and (c) all authority necessary to carry out these powers.

Section 2: Electing the President

Clause 1: Term. The President and Vice President shall serve for a term of four years. No person shall be elected President more than twice, and no person who served more than two years of another President's term under Section 3 below shall be elected President more than once.

Clause 2: Eligibility. To be elected President, a person must be a citizen born in the United States, be at least thirty-five years old, and have lived in the United States for at least fourteen years. No person ineligible to be President shall be eligible to be Vice President.

Clause 3: The Electoral College. The President shall be elected by a majority vote of the Electoral College, composed of individual Electors. Each State shall be entitled to a number of Electors equal to the total number of Representatives and Senators by which the State is represented in Congress. The District of Columbia shall be treated as if it were a state in the Electoral College, but shall not have more Electors than the least populous state. No person holding a federal office shall be appointed as an Elector.

Clause 4: Selecting the Electoral College. Each State shall decide by law the way that its electors are chosen. Congress shall dictate the time and day that the States shall choose their electors and the day that they cast their votes, but that day must be the same across the United States.

Clause 5: Selecting the President and Vice President. The Electors shall meet in their respective states and vote by separate ballots for the President and Vice President. They shall sign and certify their votes and transmit them to the President of the Senate, who shall count them in the presence of the Senate and the House of Representatives. The candidate with a majority of votes for President shall become the President-Elect; the candidate with a majority of votes for Vice President shall become the Vice-President Elect.

Clause 6: Electoral College Deadlocks. If no candidate shall earn a majority of the entire Electoral College, then the President of the Senate shall declare a deadlock. In such cases, he or she shall select the three candidates for President with the most votes and send the list to the House of Representatives. He or she shall also select the two candidates for Vice President with the most votes and send the list to the Senate.

Clause 7: Breaking a Deadlock—The President. Upon receiving the list of three candidates, the newly-elected House of Representatives shall choose the President by majority vote. However, the House shall vote by states, with each state receiving one vote. The House may not vote unless at least two-thirds of the states are represented.

Clause 8: Breaking a Deadlock—The Vice President. Upon receiving the list of two candidates, the newly-elected Senate shall choose the Vice President by majority vote. The Senate may not vote unless at least two-thirds of the Senators are present.

Clause 9: Transfer of Power. The terms of the President and Vice-President shall end on January 20th at noon, and the terms of their successors shall then begin.

Clause 10: Oath of Office. Before the President assumes office, he shall take the following oath: "I do solemnly swear (or affirm) that I will faithfully execute the office of President of the United States, and will to the best of my ability, preserve, protect and defend the Constitution of the United States."

Section 3: Presidential Succession

Clause 1: Death, Resignation, or Impeachment of the President. If the President dies, resigns, or is impeached while in office, then the Vice President shall become President.

Clause 2: Death, Ineligibility, or Lack of a President-Elect. If the President-Elect dies before his or her term begins, the Vice-President Elect shall become President. However, if the President-Elect has not been chosen or is ineligible to be President, then the Vice-President Elect shall act as President until a President is chosen or has qualified.

Clause 3: Cases Where No Person Qualifies. Congress may by law designate who shall act as President when neither a President-Elect nor a Vice-President Elect has qualified, and may by law create procedures by which a President shall be chosen. In such cases, the designated person shall be the Acting President until a President is chosen.

Clause 4: Cases Where a Candidate Dies During an Electoral College Deadlock. Congress may by law specify the procedures for choosing a President or Vice President if one of the listed candidates shall die during an Electoral College deadlock.

Clause 5: Vacancy in the Office of the Vice President. Whenever there is a vacancy in the Office of the Vice President, the President shall choose a Vice President with the consent of a majority of both houses of Congress.

Section 4: Temporary Replacement of the President

Clause 1: Voluntary Suspension. If the President concludes that he is unable to discharge the powers and duties of the office, he may send a letter to the President of the Senate and the Speaker of the House stating that inability. Until he sends them a letter to the contrary, the Vice President (or the person next in the Presidential line of succession) shall act as President.

Clause 2: Involuntary Suspension. If the Vice President and a majority of the Cabinet conclude that the President is unable to discharge the powers and duties of the office, they may send a letter to the President of the Senate and the Speaker of the House stating that inability. In such a case, the Vice President shall immediately begin acting as President.

Clause 3: Restoration of the President After Involuntary Suspension. If the President has been involuntary suspended under Clause 2, he may send the President of the Senate and the Speaker of the House of Representatives a letter saying that no inability exists. Unless the Vice President and a majority of the Cabinet send an additional letter stating otherwise within four days, the President shall be restored to office. If the restoration is contested, Congress shall meet within forty-eight hours to decide the issue. If—within twenty-one days—two-thirds of both houses of Congress determine that the President is unfit for office, the Vice President shall continue to act as President. Otherwise, the President shall be restored to office.

Section 5: The Independent Powers of the President

Clause 1: Generally. Except as stated in this section, the powers below are vested solely in the President, regardless of legislation to the contrary. When the President acts under this section, his power should be construed strictly, to prevent executive overreach.

Clause 2: Commander-in-Chief. When Congress has declared war or otherwise called the military or militia into the active service of the United States, the President shall be the Commander-in-Chief of the Army, Navy, Militia, and other military functions of the United States.

Clause 3: Foreign Relations: The President shall have power to negotiate and make treaties, but those treaties shall not be binding on the United States until ratified by two-thirds of the Senate. He or she shall also have power to open or close diplomatic relations with foreign nations, and shall represent the interests of the United States abroad.

Clause 4: Appointments. The President shall have power to appoint Ambassadors, federal judges, and all other officers of the United States whose positions are established by law, so long as the Senate approves such nominees by a majority vote. However, Congress may by law vest the power to appoint inferior officers in the President alone, in the courts, or in other appointed executive officials.

Clause 5: Recess Appointments. The President shall have power to fill vacancies without the consent of the Senate if the Senate is in recess at the time the appointment is made. However, such appointments will expire at the end of the Senate's next session.

Clause 6: Pardons. The President shall have power to grant pardons for federal crimes, except in cases of impeachment.

Clause 7: Special Sessions of Congress. The President shall have power to call special sessions of Congress in extraordinary circumstances.

Clause 8: State of the Union. The President shall, once every year, give Congress information on the State of the Union, and recommend to Congress legislation he or she judges to be necessary for the public good.

Section 6: The Concurrent Powers of the President

Clause 1: Power. When the President acts in the absence of legislation either commanding or prohibiting particular conduct, the extent of his authority must be tested by the urgency, political context, and specific facts of the situation in which the President has acted. Close cases should be resolved in favor of legality, to avoid chilling necessary action when authority is ambiguous.

Section 7: The Full Powers of the President

Clause 1: Delegation. When the President acts in obedience to the express or implied will of Congress, he acts with the full authority of the United States. In such cases, his or her action may only be set aside if the act in question violates this Constitution.

Clause 2: Enforcement. The President shall have power to enforce the laws of the United States. His or her refusal to enforce the criminal laws of the United States against an individual shall not be reviewable, by legislation or otherwise.

Clause 3: Executive Agencies. Congress may by law create executive agencies and charge them with the duty of enforcing particular laws. Once created, an agency inherits the powers and limitations of the President, and its actions may only be altered by legislation or judicial order.

Clause 4: Unlawful Actions. The Courts shall hold unlawful and set aside all executive acts that contradict this Constitution or the laws of the United States.

PART THREE
The Judicial Branch

Section 1: The Judicial Power of the United States

Clause 1: Location. The Judicial Power of the United States shall reside in the Supreme Court of the United States, and in other inferior Courts as Congress may choose to create by law.

Clause 2: Definition. The Judicial Power of the United States is the authority to conclusively decide all actual and concrete disputes that are properly placed before a federal court. When necessary to decide these disputes, the Judicial Power includes the authority to declare what the law means and to declare invalid any federal or state action contrary to this Constitution. However, the Judicial Power shall not be used to declare that the People only possess the rights listed in this Constitution.

Clause 3: Judges. Judges and Justices of the United States shall hold their offices for life unless impeached by Congress. Their salaries shall be set by law, and shall not be decreased during their time in office.

Section 2: Federal Jurisdiction

Clause 1: Limited Jurisdiction. The Judicial Power of the United States is limited to the cases and controversies listed in this Constitution. If a court discovers at any time that a case or controversy before it is not listed in this Constitution, then the court must dismiss the case or nullify any judgment entered without power to do so.

Clause 2: Federal Question Jurisdiction (Cases). Federal courts may exercise jurisdiction over the following cases:
- (a) Any case that could present a legal issue involving this Constitution, or the laws or treaties made by Congress under the Constitution's authority;
- (b) All cases affecting ambassadors and foreign diplomats;
- (c) All cases of admiralty and maritime law; and
- (d) All criminal prosecutions brought by the United States.

Clause 3: Diversity Jurisdiction (Controversies). Federal courts may exercise jurisdiction over the following controversies:
- (a) All cases between two or more States;
- (b) Any case where opposing parties are citizens of different States; and
- (c) All cases between citizens of the same state who claim ownership of land granted by different States.

Clause 4: Supplemental Jurisdiction. If a federal court exercises jurisdiction under Clauses 2 or 3, it may also exercise jurisdiction over other claims that arise out of the same factual pattern, even if the court would be unable the exercise jurisdiction over that claim standing alone.

Clause 5: Jurisdiction of the Supreme Court. In all cases affecting ambassadors, foreign diplomats, and in lawsuits between States, the Supreme Court shall have original and exclusive jurisdiction. In all other cases mentioned above, the Supreme Court may exercise appellate jurisdiction to review decisions of state and federal courts. Congress may, by law, create exceptions and regulations to this jurisdiction. Congress shall not expand the original jurisdiction of the Supreme Court.

Clause 6: Standing. No federal court shall hear a dispute unless the party seeking federal jurisdiction proves that:
- (a) It has suffered (or will soon suffer) a concrete and specific harm;
- (b) That harm is fairly traceable to the defendant's actions; and
- (c) A favorable decision would remedy the harm.

Clause 7: Ripeness. No federal court shall hear a dispute if the harm alleged is so speculative that the benefits of waiting for a more concrete dispute outweigh the hardship to the parties of withholding review.

Clause 8: Mootness. No federal court shall continue to hear a dispute if a crucial issue in the case is no longer in dispute or if the court can no longer grant the relief the party seeks. However, this clause shall not apply to cases where (1) the harm alleged could be repeated but would be moot by the time the party could be fairly heard; or (2) the defendant voluntarily stops the harmful behavior but is free to start it again.

Clause 9: Political Questions. No federal court shall hear a case or controversy if it consists entirely of political disputes better addressed to elected officials. These disputes include, but are not limited to, claims that a State has been deprived of a republican form of government; the President's foreign-policy decisions; the internal rules of Congress; the process for ratifying amendments; impeachments; and all other cases where the legal rights of individuals are not at stake.

Section 3: The Rights of Parties

Clause 1: Criminal Investigations. The people shall have the right to be free from all unreasonable government searches and seizures of their bodies, homes, documents, and property. Searches and seizures conducted with a warrant are always reasonable if the warrant is issued by a neutral judge, is supported by probable cause and facts given under oath, and specifically describes the place to be searched or the person or things to be seized.

Clause 2: Criminal Cases. In all criminal prosecutions, whether brought by a State or by the United States, the person accused shall have the following rights:
- (a) <u>Speedy & Public Trials.</u> The right to a speedy and public trial, by an impartial jury of the State and district where the crime was committed. Such districts shall be previously created by law. Congress shall direct by law the location of a trial if the crime is not committed within any State.
- (b) <u>Notice.</u> The right to know the crime and the underlying facts that he or she is accused of committing.
- (c) <u>Confrontation.</u> The right to confront and cross-examine any witnesses against him or her.
- (d) <u>Subpoena</u>. The right to use the Court's power to compel the attendance of witnesses in his or her favor.
- (e) <u>Lawyers.</u> The right to bring a lawyer to court for his or her defense, and, if he or she cannot afford a lawyer, the right to have the government provide one at public expense.
- (f) <u>Self-Incrimination</u>: The right not to testify against himself or herself.

- (g) <u>Double Jeopardy</u>: The right, once a jury has been chosen, to have an acquittal be conclusive and unreviewable by any court.
- (h) <u>Cruel and Unusual Punishment</u>: The right not to be subjected to bail, fines, or punishment that are inhumane, cruel, malicious, disproportionate, or so barbaric that they cannot be tolerated in a free country.
- (i) <u>Interpretation of Criminal Laws.</u> The right to have ambiguous criminal laws interpreted in their favor, so that the government may not impose criminal punishment for conduct not clearly prohibited.

Clause 3: The Grand Jury. The federal government shall not charge someone with a capital crime or a felony until that person has been indicted by a federal Grand Jury. This clause shall not apply in cases arising in the Military, or in cases involving the Militia when it is called into actual service.

Clause 4: Eminent Domain. Neither the United States nor any State shall seize private property except for public use. If the government does seize property for public use, it must pay the owner the fair value of the property.

Clause 5: Due Process. Neither the United States nor any State shall deprive any specific person of their life, liberty, or property without giving that person notice and an opportunity to be heard in front of a neutral decision-maker. In other cases, such a person may be entitled to additional protections, if the significance of the right and the risk of its loss under existing protections is greater than the burden on the government of providing more protection.

Clause 6: Civil Lawsuits. In all civil controversies brought under a federal court's diversity jurisdiction, the parties shall have the right to trial by jury. This jury's findings of fact shall not be reexamined in any federal court unless the losing party can prove that a legal error improperly influenced the jury or that the verdict was against the weight of the evidence.

Section 4: Treason

Clause 1: Definition. No person shall be charged with Treason against the United States unless they have (1) committed an act of war against the United States; or (2) sworn allegiance to an enemy of the United States and given them assistance.

Clause 2: Evidence. No person shall be convicted of Treason unless (1) two witnesses testify to the same overt act; or (2) the accused confesses under oath in open court.

Clause 3: Punishment. Congress shall have power to pass laws declaring the punishment for Treason. However, no conviction for treason shall impose a legal disability on the convict's family, nor shall it be used to seize property except during the life of the person convicted.

PART FOUR
Federalism

Section 1: Federal Supremacy

Clause 1: Citizenship. Every person born or naturalized in the United States is a citizen of the United States and of the state where they live.

Clause 2: Supremacy of Federal Law. This Constitution, in addition to the laws and treaties made under its authority, are the supreme law of the land. All laws contrary to federal law are void.

Clause 3: Supremacy of Federal Debt. When legally incurred, the public debt of the United States shall not be questioned.

Clause 4: Illegal Debts. The United States shall not pay any debt incurred by a state in rebellion against the United States, and it shall not compensate any person for the loss or emancipation of any slave. All such debts and claims are illegal.

Clause 5: Supporting the Constitution. All federal and state officers shall give an oath to support this Constitution. No person shall serve as a public official in the federal government or the government of any state if they took this oath and then participated in a rebellion against the United States. However, Congress may remove this disability by a two-thirds vote of both houses. No religious test shall be required to hold public office.

Section 2: Guarantees to the States

Clause 1: Sovereign Immunity. No state or federal court shall permit a person to file a lawsuit for damages against any State unless the State consents. However, Congress may by law expressly remove this immunity when protecting individual rights.

Clause 2: Discrimination Among States. Neither Congress nor any State shall pass a commercial or regulatory law favoring one state over another.

Clause 3: Full Faith & Credit. All States shall recognize and give full effect to the public records and judicial orders of every other State. Congress may determine by law the records and orders subject to this clause's guarantees.

Clause 4: Extradition. On the request of the Governor of a State, any person who is charged with a crime in that State and is found in another, shall be arrested by the state where he or she is found and returned to the state with jurisdiction over the crime.

Clause 5: Federal Protection. Congress shall ensure that every State has a representative form of government, shall protect them from invasion, and (at the request of the legislature or the governor) shall protect them against rebellions within the State.

PART FIVE
Amendments

Section 1: Admission to the Union

Clause 1: Procedure. Congress may by law admit new states into the Union.

Clause 2: Prohibitions. Unless both Congress and the relevant states agree, no new state shall: (a) be formed within any other state, or (b) be formed by merging two or more states.

Section 2: Amending the Constitution

Clause 1: Proposal. Amendments to this Constitution may be proposed by (a) two-thirds of both Houses of Congress, or (b) a Convention of the states.

Clause 2: Convention Procedure. When two-thirds of state legislatures pass resolutions requesting a convention for proposing Amendments, Congress shall convene a Convention of state delegates for proposing Amendments.

Clause 3: Ratification. A proposed Amendment shall become a binding and enforceable part of this Constitution when three-fourths of the state legislatures or conventions ratify it.

Manufactured by Amazon.com
Columbia, SC
10 April 2017